# Temple Manor

STROOD, ROCHESTER, KENT

## S E RIGOLD  MA, FSA

*formerly Principal Inspector of Ancient Monuments*

*The surviving building, a house of the Knights Templar, comprises a thirteenth-century structure of stone with a seventeenth-century brick extension at either end, but it must not be imagined that this represents the complete dwelling at any period. As originally built it was indeed detached – there are windows on all sides and no trace of any other building having been joined to it. However, it must be envisaged as part of the court that we know existed by 1185, a complex of timber structures, hall, kitchens, barns, and stables, to which the stone one was added in about 1240.*

*After the time of the Templars, but before the brick extensions were built, there were already several enlargements on the north side: in the fourteenth century a ground-floor hall was added, which later became a kitchen, and in the fifteenth century a timber-framed wing, jettied on two sides and providing a spacious parlour on the ground floor on the west.*

# CONTENTS

*Visit our website at www.english-heritage.org.uk*

© *English Heritage 1970*
*First published 1962*
*First published by English Heritage 1970*
*1 Waterhouse Square, 138–142 Holborn, London, EC1N 2ST*
*Reprinted 2010, 2015*
*Printed in England by Purbrooks Ltd*
*C10 10/15 00014*

ISBN 978 1 85074 302 6

**Front cover:** *Temple Manor from the north-west, showing the 17th-century western extension*

**Back cover:** *View from the south*

# DESCRIPTION

*This view of the northern side shows the later extensions added to both ends of the Templars' thirteenth-century building. The modern external stairs follow the line of the original medieval stairs and give access to the first-floor hall*

The surviving building comprises a thirteenth-century structure of stone with a seventeenth-century brick extension at either end, but it must not be imagined that this represents the complete dwelling at any period.

As originally built it was indeed detached – there are windows on all sides and no trace of any other building having been joined to it. However, it must be envisaged as part of the *curia* or court that we know existed by 1185, a complex of timber structures, hall, kitchens, barns, and stables, to which the stone one was added in about 1240.

After the time of the Templars, but before the brick extensions were built, there were already several enlargements on the north side: in the fourteenth century a

ground-floor hall was added, which later became a kitchen, and in the fifteenth century a timber-framed wing, jettied on two sides and providing a spacious parlour on the ground floor at the west end. The entrance was at the corner where the existing brick porch and stair turret were later placed, and gave easy access to all parts of the house, including the cellarage in the old undercroft.

At a later date an attic floor was inserted in the old hall, its walls were breached in two places and finally the house was divided into two dwellings. The additions on the north side, which had been much remodelled, as well as all internal partitions and floors inserted into the hall, have now been removed. The south side has been unencumbered at all periods.

## The stone building

This is of ragstone and flint rubble, with accurate and sometimes elaborately moulded ashlar details and shafts of Purbeck marble. It is a respectable example of early thirteenth-century architecture, on two floors – a high upper storey and a low vaulted undercroft. It has generally been classed with the early medieval stone houses of normal pattern called 'first-floor halls,' in which the main room, for eating and all communal activities, is raised above the undercroft (cellar) and approached by an external staircase.

It is far from typical: there is no communication between the undercroft and the hall above, no internal division on either floor and no obvious domestic conveniences. For this reason some have claimed that it was not a dwelling but a chapel, quoting as a parallel a very similar building, demolished in 1960, on a site of the Knights Hospitaller at Moor Hall, Middlesex. But in fact neither building had the distinctive fittings of a chapel, and the eastern part of Temple Manor, which in that case would be the sanctuary, is less ornate than the west. Nor is it likely that the tenants of the pious Countess of Pembroke would have been allowed to convert a chapel into a house.

The probable reason for both buildings, in each of which the better lit eastern third was screened off from the rest, is that they were for the accommodation of a dignitary in transit rather than for permanent habitation and were the buildings designated *camerae* or chambers, comparable with those for the private accommodation of great personages at royal and episcopal palaces. At Moor Hall, and probably also at Temple Manor, there was also a proper ground-floor hall. The upper floor was divided into two by a light timber screen: the inner chamber was for privacy (though it is possible that it also served as a chapel) and the outer was for the conduct of public business and for people awaiting attendance, who would have sat on the stone seats round the walls. One piece of evidence from Moor Hall is relevant: it is quite likely that Temple Manor also had three lancets in the east wall.

The habitable upper floor was approached by an external staircase, similar to, but not quite on the lines of, the reconstructed one. Traces of its supporting posts, which were reset in the same positions when the range was added on the north side, have been discovered; their positions are now marked on the ground. The single entrance has a richly moulded arched head. The numerous but accurately fitted voussoirs and the Purbeck marble shafts, flanked by hollow chamfers with bar stops, are in the best Early English manner.

There are holes for a light drawbar just inside the door. The actual door is modern. It opens into the outer chamber, which was open to the roof and lit by a single lancet at the west and by three lateral lancets. These were set in the wall arcades of three arches on the north and five on the south, rising from continuous seats and originally provided with Purbeck marble shafts, like the doorway. These arcades were much mutilated, particularly by breaches in the north wall, and have been partly restored; their eastern terminations are not exactly opposite each other. The wall plaster, both within and above the arches, was painted with imitation ashlar joints, a common thirteenth-century practice. There are graffiti scratched on the plaster, such as boats, patterns made with compasses and a name (Cray?).

There was no wall fireplace, but a portable brazier or a stone hearth could safely have been placed on the floor of mixed clay and lime, covering the vault below. Just before the Templars surrendered it this floor was probably tiled,

# FIRST FLOOR

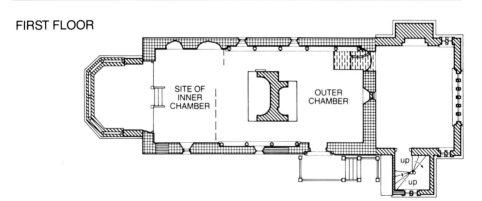

# GROUND FLOOR

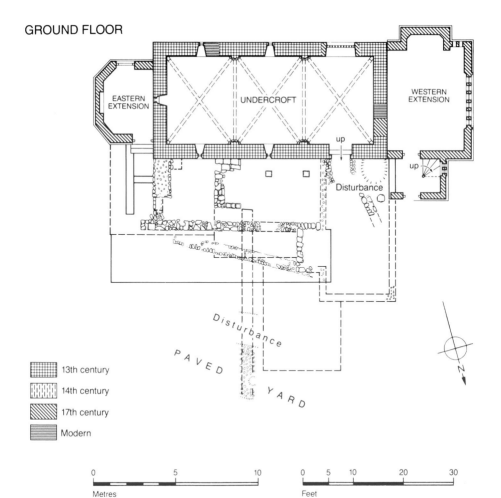

*The upper floor of the thirteenth-century house of the Knights Templar. This floor was probably used as lodgings by important Templar officials journeying along the London–Dover road. The fireplace is a seventeenth-century addition*

as many scattered tiles of this date, some inlaid with foliage patterns, have been discovered.

In the area of the inner chamber, which now gives directly on to the seventeenth-century brick oriel, few features remain. There are a mutilated string course on the east wall and traces of a change of plan on the south. It was evidently intended to have a window opposite that on the north, but this was replaced by two splayed recesses, one going down to ground-floor level; neither pierces the wall as a window, and neither is of the right dimensions for an ecclesiastical piscina nor for a proper garderobe chamber. It is possible they are part of an internal screened-off garderobe: the shorter recess may have been for a washbasin such as occasionally occurs in well-fitted medieval chambers, and a course of stones on the exterior wall may indicate the shoot of

garderobe fitted into a the longer one.

In the post-medieval period the floor level was raised to that of the arcade seat, and a loft floor was inserted, lit by windows still traceable in the gables. A massive brick chimneystack was inserted, with fireplaces at both levels, which has been allowed to remain. The wooden lintels in the fireplaces are rougher than that in the western extension, though the chimney top and the gables, which formerly had a curved Dutch outline, must belong to that build. The roof is entirely reconstructed; its predecessor, which collapsed in 1949, was an affair of plain coupled rafters, and might, in part, have survived from the original building.

In the southwest corner is a curious sinking in the floor, with a drain leading into the west wall, in which are remains of an arched oven in tiles inserted into a

*The thirteenth-century undercroft. This room would have been used for storage, and access was by the single doorway at the western end of the north wall*

segmental-headed ashlar hatch in the wall. The latter is probably an early feature, allowing access for food, etc, but not for people, from some destroyed outbuilding to the west, rather than an extra fireplace to the extension. The purpose of the later oven or still is uncertain. Its floor, of worn and burned reused early fourteenth-century tiles, was well below the raised floor level of the room.

## The undercroft

This is entered by a plain arch. The three bays of quadripartite ribbed vaults are intact (see page 7). The squared chalk filling between the ribs is excellent, but the simple chamfering of the ribs and the capitals of the semi-circular responds contrasts with the more elaborate ornaments of the hall.

The windows, remarkably wide for an undercroft, have their original internal oak lintels, giving a square head, fitted into a pointed external surround. The windows had vertical iron bars. There is a repaired breach in the west wall and the long southwest window, with many diagonal mullions, is an alteration of the seventeenth century. At all periods the undercroft was merely a cellar.

## The western extension

This dates from the second quarter of the seventeenth century. It is of neat English-bond brickwork, with moulded string courses and squared fillets round the windows. These were originally rendered in mortar to simulate ashlar dressings – a local mannerism of the period.

The extension consists of three storeys,

*Temple Manor from the south, showing the original thirteenth-century building with later extensions at both ends*

each of one fine room, very well lit, particularly on the west. There is a stair turret, incorporating a porch, on the north; the east wall of this is a mere partition, as the staircase also served buildings that stood on the east of it.

The woodwork is good, though nothing remains of the original staircase. The doors have ovolo mouldings. The main beam of the ground-floor ceiling is quite ornate, with a sunken half-round along its centre; that of the first-floor ceiling has an ovolo, carried round the cornice.

On the first floor the fireplace is mutilated but contains traces of an oven; that on the ground floor is impressive, with its massive timber lintel forming a low four-centred arch. Beside each fireplace is a small two-light window. There is no fireplace in the attic, but the chimney has three flues.

The whole block comprises an elegant and relatively independent apartment, perhaps for the older generation of Blakes (see page 13), while the rest of the family and servants occupied the old house.

## The eastern extension

This is rather later, probably dating from the third quarter of the seventeenth century. The brickwork is less regular and the mouldings at cornice level are different from those at the other end, and more classical in feeling.

The ornamental timber modillions supporting the eaves, with a lozenge pattern on the 'plate' between them, are original, and taken with the classicising mouldings of the rest suggest a local interpretation of fashions set by Inigo Jones and his colleagues. Though the present form of the large gazebo-like upper window, with sashes and glazing bars, is later, its predecessor, a continuous mullioned window, which still existed in 1767, gave a similar wide view over the river – now spoilt by the railway and the industrial estate. This outlook seems the main purpose of the extension – the chamber below was just an office or store. There are, however, footings of an earlier structure at this end, perhaps contemporary with the western extension.

# HISTORY

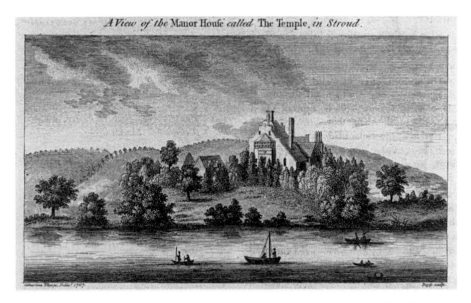

*A View of the Manor House called The Temple, in Strood.*

*Temple Manor in 1767, an engraving after a drawing by Catherine Thorpe, in Hasted's 'History of Kent'*

The manor of 'Strood Temple' comprised the greater part of the parish of Strood, but most of the built-up area of the town lay outside it. This smaller area, the bridgehead opposite Rochester, belonged to the monks of the cathedral and contained an important hospital known as the Newark or New Work, sometimes wrongly confused with the Templars' establishment.

The larger area remained a royal manor until King Henry II, early in his reign, in 1159 at latest, gave it to the Knights Templar, with the dues and administrative rights of the Hundred of Shamel in which it lay. This was one of the ancient sub-divisions of the county and lay along the west bank of the Medway but excluded the urban part of Strood. The manor, of course, was not merely the manor house

and the demesne, or home farm, that supplied it, but a whole complex of rights to services, payments and minor jurisdictions, which if well managed, could bring a considerable profit.

## Knights Templar

These were an order of celibate soldiers, living under a stern monastic discipline and established in the Holy Land during the crusading period, in order to protect the Holy Places and the pilgrims resorting to them.

When in 1128, the Pope confirmed their first rule (modelled on the Cistercian), he exempted them from interference by bishops or other ecclesiastical functionaries, except their own, in all parts of Christendom. They were even immune from interdicts such as were laid upon England in the time of King John. Such privileges caused deep jealously on the part of the established clergy, and the Templars' notorious solidarity and secretiveness only made matters worse.

In the Holy Land the Templars fought valiantly and their castles were the main bulwark of the Christian states founded there. They also acquired extensive possessions everywhere in Europe, the profits of which were intended to be devoted to their cause. But much of their energy was soon being spent in administering these estates with an efficiency and security which transformed the Templars into an extremely rich international power.

Many persons, from kings downwards, became obliged to the Templars for loans of money, safeguarding valuables, management of business (Henry III's High Almoner was a Templar) and worldwide contacts. Both King Stephen, who established them in England, and his rivals, the Empress Matilda and her son, later Henry II, were in their debt by the time their struggles were over, and it was probably in consideration of this that Henry gave them Strood. Apart from its value as an estate, it was coveniently placed, near the main road to the Continent, for Templars to lodge in when travelling on business.

A house where the Templars lived the regular life was called a Preceptory or Commandery. Strood never reached this dignity, except possibly at the very end of its existence. There was but one Preceptory in Kent, at Ewell, near Dover, founded by Henry II's brother William and several knights who had an interest in lands just north of Strood and owed service at Dover Castle. It seems as though Ewell, Strood, and an estate at Deal, which is always associated with it, were effectively parts of the same donation. A few years later the

Templars acquired Denny, in Cambridgeshire, where a monastery recently founded had not proved a success and its buildings were used as a kind of infirmary for retired Templars. This house was later to have its destiny linked with that of Strood.

There were never more than about a hundred and fifty Templars in England to manage some eighty preceptories and manors and hundreds of smaller estates. Of these not more than a tenth – only six in 1308 – were knights; the rest were sergeants or brethren, clerks rather than warriors, of less gentle birth, but united by a pride in their administrative profession, rare, even alarming, in the Middle Ages. Thus a preceptor was seldom a knight, and in a manor such as Strood it is unlikely that even two brethren would have been permanently in residence. The likelihood is that they installed a lay reeve (local official) or bailiff.

Although a great survey of their English estates was made for the King in 1185, giving full details about the sub-tenants in Strood, the Templars' secretiveness has left little documentation about individual houses. It is not known precisely when or why the fine stone building in Strood was built, some seventy years after they had acquired the manor. The probable reason is that it was to provide more splendid lodging for Templar dignitaries (such as the Royal Almoner), while travelling from London to Dover (they even had a private postal service on this road). A simpler house on another site would have sufficed for the reeve.

The high finish of building symbolises the Templars' wealth that was still increasing in the middle of the thirteenth century – nine new houses were added to those recorded in 1185. King John and Henry III in their troubled reigns became increasingly indebted to them and repaid their obligations with a further charter of privileges including a tax-free representative in every borough. The Templars remained aloof, hated and respected, even when the reason for their existence had ceased with the loss of the last Christian foothold in Palestine in 1291.

## Suppression of the Templars

In 1307 King Philip IV of France, a calculating monster, having just confiscated the possessions of the Jews in his realm, decided to seize those of the Templars. The long-standing jealousy on the part of the secular clergy and the burgesses gave him moral support; so did the secrecy of the Templars' methods which had already raised scandals in the public imagination.

Accordingly all the Templars in France were arrested and accused of compromising with Islam, of sexual irregularities and of other misdemeanours, some quite fantastic.

The Pope at first protested and tried to keep the trial in his own courts and then to close it, but being practically a pensioner of the King, he was forced to support him and send legates to make the other sovereigns follow the same policy.

In 1308 the English Templars were imprisoned. Their treatment was lenient until the legate pointed to the widespread confessions produced by ruthlessness and torture in France. The weak Edward II then countenanced the use of torture, against all the practice of English Common Law, but the English officials on the whole showed an admirable restraint in the face of this hysterical provocation: William Greenfield, Archbishop of York, in particular, forbade torture in his jurisdiction and secured protection and provision for the victims.

In France many Templars were executed, including, at last, the Grand Master himself, still protesting his innocence. In England nobody was put to death, though the Grand Preceptor died in prison. In 1312 the Order was dissolved throughout Christendom. At the same time the Pope did something to regularise the sordid affair and to deprive Philip of his spoil by insisting that the Templars' possessions should go to the rival Military Order, the Knights Hospitaller, who still had their proper function to perform. The lay authorities were slow to comply with this: in Portugal the King, by endowing a new order, practically re-established the Templars under another name, and Edward II, who like his French father-in-law had been enjoying their revenues since 1308, only handed the lands over to the Hospitallers at the end of 1313.

There exists an inventory of Templar estates (including Strood) and their contents when they were in the King's hands. Strood possessed a hall, a chamber, a chapel and a barn. From 1313 Strood (though not the Hundred of Shamel, which had been transferred to the great local family of Cobham in 1241) theoretically belonged to the Hospitallers. Whether they drew any rent from it is doubtful, as a few years later their Grand Prior complained that the King was still occupying, or had reoccupied, certain Templar estates including Denny and Strood.

This state of affairs was regularised in 1324 when the prior formally ceded them to the King, but fifteen years later his successor, in his return sent to the Grand Master of the Order at his headquarters on the island of Rhodes, was still unwilling to admit it as final. About this period some of the scattered timber buildings that had served the needs of the early medieval manor at Strood were pulled down, leaving the stone hall as the nucleus of a compact house, as the new fashion demanded.

Archaeological evidence suggests that occupation continued undisturbed by these disputes. Whoever enjoyed the revenue, it seems probable that it was already converted into a farm, and possible that the tenants were the Creyes, who, although they were the wealthiest family in Strood, held no land there in direct feudal tenure.

## Subsequent history

In 1336 Edward III granted the former Templars' house at Denny to his kinswoman, Mary of St Pol, Countess of Pembroke. A devout woman, widowed young, she used her wealth and influence in good works. In particular she tried to bring about conciliation between the warring kingdoms of England and France, probably using the status of a Franciscan Tertiary to give her something like diplomatic immunity.

Besides founding Pembroke College, Cambridge, the Countess refounded Denny as a house of Franciscan nuns and a place of retirement for herself. In 1342, when she was transferring the nuns to Denny, the King granted her Strood Temple as an endowment for any religious house she pleased. Two years later she gave it to Denny.

It was too distant to provide produce for the nunnery and there is little doubt that it continued as before, put out to farm for money. We know nothing of the actual inhabitants, except that they gradually enlarged the house to give more comfort and privacy. First, early in the fourteenth century, a ground-floor hall was attached, parallel to the stone building, and then in the fifteenth century a timber wing was added by its side, and the great barn was rebuilt (all these additions have been removed).

There is no reason to suppose that the farmers were greatly disturbed by the changes of ownership that followed the dissolution of Denny Abbey. Because the nuns were unusually well connected they staved off the inevitable surrender to the officers of Henry VIII until relatively late,

but by 1539 Strood had been granted to the same man, one Elrington, as Denny. He promptly sold it to the Cobhams, who had long held the Hundred of Shamel.

In 1603 the then Lord Cobham, his brother and others, including Sir Walter Raleigh, were convicted of an alleged conspiracy against James I. Some were executed, then or later, and all forfeited their estates. The chief agent in this undoing (not without help from Cobham, who tried to save himself by further implicating the others) was the crafty Robert Cecil, soon to become Earl of Salisbury and Lord High Treasurer. Among his share of the spoils were the Hundred of Shamel and Strood Temple (though it had originally been among the lands reserved in trust for Cobham's wife, Lady Kildare); these he or his son sold piecemeal when a good market arose.

Thus Temple Manor passed, by way of a London lawyer called Hyde, to the Stuart Duke of Richmond, a relative of the King. He had acquired Cobham Hall after Lady Kildare's death and was busy reassembling the forfeited estates when the Civil War threatened and he hurriedly disposed of Temple Manor to one Isaac Blake (or Blaque – a spelling borrowed from a dean of Rochester who was no relation).

The Blakes had probably been the sitting tenants for some years; they were then perhaps the richest family in Strood and, as actual inhabitants, much more relevant to the Manor House than the grandees who held it 'in chief.' Isaac appears in the churchwardens' accounts of Strood as churchwarden himself, and as dealing in ironware, perhaps also in scrap iron. It is interesting to note that quantities of miscellaneous broken ironwork, including cannon balls, were excavated in one dump at Temple Manor.

The Blakes refashioned the high gables in the Dutch mode and added the two brick extensions to the old house on two different occasions, thus symbolising their climb in status from tradesmen to petty gentry. Whereas ordinary folk lived in timber-framed buildings, fashionable brickwork, at least where it could be seen, gave the house an air of quality. The Blakes sold it in the eighteenth century, but their various successors were generally people of the same sort, combining farming with commerce and including a family that established the local brick-making industry.

The great nineteenth-century antiquary C Roach Smith did not live here, but at Temple Place, a small estate carved out of the large farm, which was beginning to be dismembered in the cause of industry and rising population. Nevertheless Temple Farm remained well cared for and fairly isolated in a fine garden until the early 1930s, when, unfortunately for the outlook from Temple Manor, the City of Rochester acquired what was left of the estate for industrial development.

Seeking a use that might preserve the house, which was destined to be surrounded by factories, the city authorities in 1934 consulted the well-known architect Sir Herbert Baker, and approached His Majesty's Office of Works. Finally, in 1938, when no economic use had been found, a local committee was formed to preserve it. Unfortunately their efforts were interrupted by the war, and when, late in 1950, the city offered it in guardianship to what is now the Department of the Environment, twelve years of neglect and hooliganism had done their worst.

The great barn had come down, the roof had collapsed and the timber wing was considered beyond repair. Early in 1951 the work of repair was taken in hand. Rather than to rebuild the wing, it was decided to reconstruct the external staircase, approximately as it was before the first timber additions were made. The area where these stood was then excavated, but the footings found were too flimsy to expose, and after the house had been consolidated the area was grassed.

# GLOSSARY

**Ashlar** Squared blocks of stone; dressed masonry of large blocks laid in regular courses with fine joints

**Chamfer** Bevelled or mitred edge, formed by cutting off the arris usually at 45 degrees

**Draw bar** Bar to secure a door or gate from the inside.

**Fillets** Flat bands of masonry or brickwork, projected slightly from the wall

**Garderobe** Latrine usually flushed by a channel of water or by discharging into a cesspit or through an outer wall

**Gazebo** Small building, raised above a wall, from which a view can be obtained

**In chief** See *Land held in chief*

**Jettied** Timber-framed upper storey resting on joists and projecting beyond the lower storey

**Lancet** Narrow, single-light, pointed window, characteristic of the thirteenth-century

**Land held in chief** Land held directly from the Crown, mainly by barons but sometimes by knights

**Modillon** Small bracket supporting a cornice or projecting course at the top of a wall

**Ovolo** Convex moulding of quarter-circle or quarter-ellipse section, receding downwards

**Piscina** Basin with a drain in a wall niche near the altar, for washing sacramental vessels

**Quadripartite** Said of a vault, where the intersecting ribs divide each bay into four segments (as distinct from six)

**Ragstone** A limy sandstone from the Greensand series – one of Kent's few natural building stones

**Reeve** Bailiff, steward or overseer; local official of minor rank

**Rib** Projecting band of stone, part of a framework, structurally supporting a vaulted roof

**Rubble** Unshaped stones, used for rougher walling

**Shaft** Part of a column between base and capital; often one of a group of two or more clustered columns of lesser diameter; small or subordinate pillar

**String course** Horizontal band of masonry projecting noticeably and usually moulded

**Tertiary** Lay person, living 'in the world' under a modified version of the rule of the Franciscan friars

**Undercroft** Vaulted room or cellar supporting a principal chamber above

**Vault** Stone ceiling (or imitation), usually arched for structural strength, and sometimes relieved by stone ribs. *Barrel vault*, arched semicylindrical vault; tunnel vault

**Voussoir** Wedge-shaped stone forming part of an arch